Darling
PRESS

Garbage Truck Book

For Kids Who Love to Learn About Trash Trucks with Real Photos

Garbage trucks help clean our streets. They pick up garbage every day!

There are many types of garbage trucks. They can load from the front, back, or side.

The garbage truck's big arms lift the garbage bin. Then the trash gets dumped into the truck.

Sometimes if you wave to the garbage truck driver they'll honk the horn for you. Try it next time you see one!

Some garbage trucks play music, like in Japan. Some garbage trucks sort trash, like in Europe.

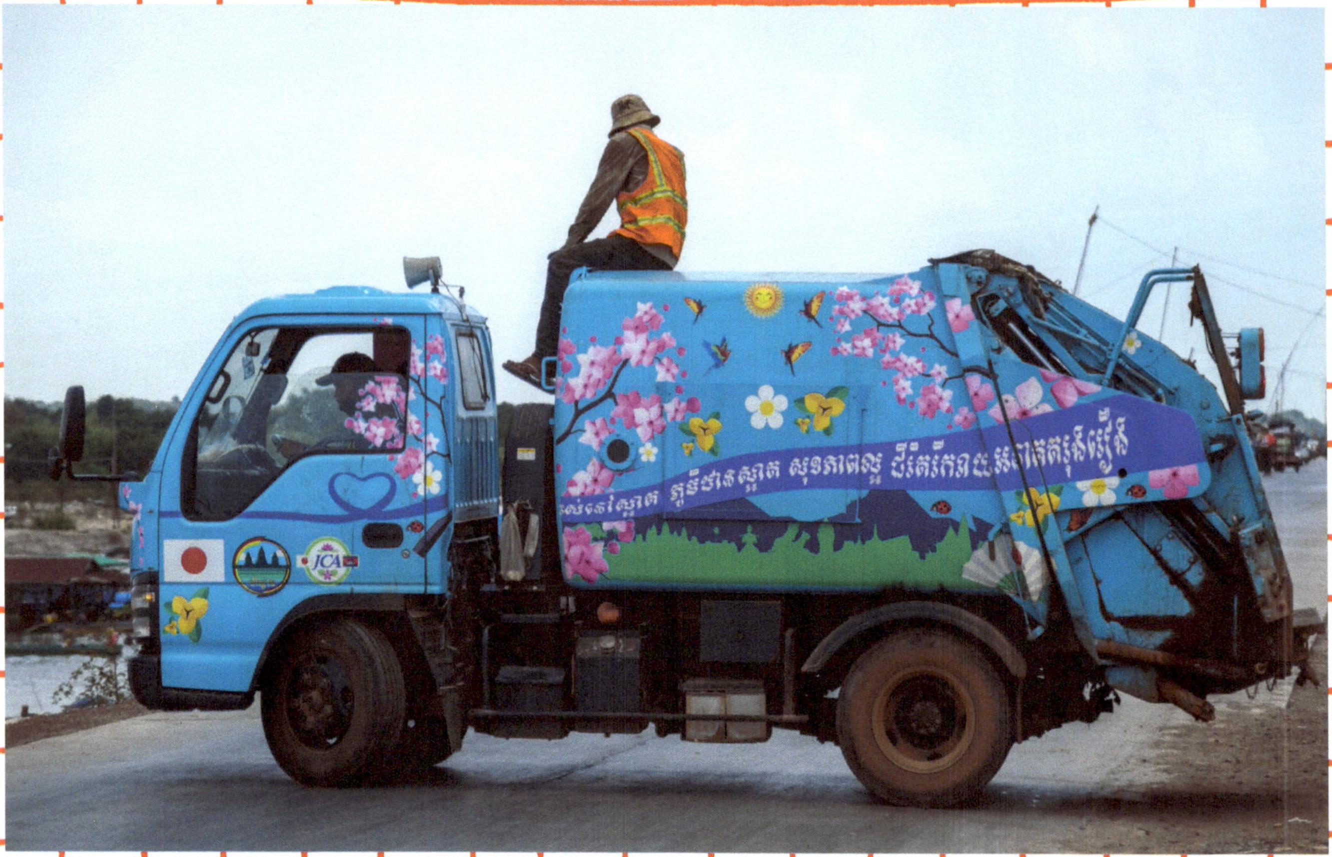

Garbage trucks have a very important job. They carry tons of trash and keep the streets of the world clean.

Long ago people had to carry their trash by hand or use horse-drawn carriages.

GARBAGE STRIKE — CART BEING STONED — DRIVER IS INSIDE

Some garbage trucks have something called a compactor that squishes all the trash. This makes room for more.

Once the garbage trucks collect all of the trash, they go to a place where all the trash gets sorted or a landfill.

When's the next time your trash will get picked up?

Maybe you can wave to the driver and see if they will honk the horn for you.

Some garbage trucks have helper people who ride on the back of the truck. These people help grab the garbage bins.

What are some sounds the
garbage truck can make?

HONK HONK
(hello/ look-out!)

VROOM!
(I'm fast!)

BEEP BEEP BEEP
(I'm backing up!)

What kind of garbage bins do you have? (trash, recycling, compost, etc.) Can you put one piece of trash away where it goes?

BYE BYE, garbage truck. Thank you for keeping our streets clean and see you next time!

THE END

goodbye

www.ingramcontent.com/pod-product-compliance
Lightning Source LLC
Chambersburg PA
CBHW060836270326
41933CB00002B/106